I0472557

Photoshop
From Beginner to Pro In Less than 1 Day - Step By Step Guide to Learning the Basics In No Time

(Digital Photography, Graphic Design, Photo Editing)

by James Clark

Table of Contents

Photoshop

Disclaimer

While all attempts have been made to verify the information provided in this book, the author does not assume any responsibility for errors, omissions, or contrary interpretations of the subject matter contained within. The information provided in this book is for educational and entertainment purposes only. The reader is responsible for his or her own actions and the author does not accept any responsibilities for any liabilities or damages, real or perceived, resulting from the use of this information.

Introduction

Photoshop is a powerful photo editing tool that will bring your digital photography to the next level. There are many things you can accomplish with photoshop and learning how does not have to be complicated.

The digital photography tools in photoshop can turn a photo into a work of art, create the perfect images for a web page, and remove flaws from images while changing the lighting and reducing blur.

As you work through the chapters in this book you will learn the how to use all of the features photoshop has to offer.

Digital editing is more than fixing flawed pictures, digital editing includes digital video and working with 3D elements.

Photoshop does more than fix pictures and this book covers everything from beginner techniques to advanced digital editing.

There are many facets to photoshop, once you learn the basics, you will move on to more advanced techniques.

Learning how to use photoshop for video editing will provide you with powerful tools you can use to turn your amateur videos into a stunning masterpiece. You can use photoshop to clean up your video and add professional touches and effects.

Photoshop templates are perfect for designing web pages and keeping things consistent across the page or for creating awesome scrapbook pages and other print media.

Templates provide you with a layout that you just fill in with your images. You will learn how to create your own templates, save them, and use them.

Layers can appear complicated to first time photoshop users. You will learn how to effectively work with layers and improve your digital editing skills. Layers seem complicated but once you learn how and why they are used, the rest is a piece of cake.

Layers do more than help you create awesome images, they help you keep track of your changes.

Photoshop filters can change everything about your image. The right filter can turn a photo into a work of art. If you know a bit about photography, you have heard about lenses filters.

Photoshop filters make similar changes and a whole lot more. You can use filters to change a color image to black and white and that's just the beginning.

The skills you will gain from this book will help give you everything you need to use Adobe Photoshop to achieve professional results. This book demystifies Photoshop and gives you the simple explanations you need to become proficient with this program.

Nothing is too hard or too advanced if you understand how it works.

Chapter 1 – Conquer the Basics

Learning to use the basic tools in Photoshop will provide the ground work for just about everything else you will learn to do. Knowledge of the basics will give you everything you need work through your first project with Photoshop.

Instead of learning using one of your own digital images, try searching for an image provided by Adobe Stock.

Using Adobe Stock Images and Video

Adobe Stock images are images you can access through the creative cloud, you can save these images to libraries for later use and when you are ready to use them you just click to license them. Adobe Stock images have watermarks, these watermarks are removed as soon as you click to license them.

Stock images are:

- Used for web and print projects

- Licensed for use through Adobe Stock

Stock images have a multitude of uses. Web page graphic designers may use stock images to create web pages. They can be used for print ads and other publications that require images.

Stock images can be used according to their license; licensing ensures the individuals who created the image are compensated.

To work with an Adobe Stock image, open Photoshop and click open the libraries panel. Select Adobe Stock from the menu then enter search criteria in the search box. When you find the image, you want to use you can find more details about the image by right clicking and click view details on the web.

You can right click to license and save the image to your library or you can view the preview of the image, the preview has a watermark.

You can save the preview or continue searching for similar images in your own libraries or Adobe Stock. When you decide on an image you want to use, right click and license the image to remove the watermark.

When you are ready to work with the image, double click it to open it in a workspace, or click and drag it to your workspace. You can also search for Adobe Stock Video in the libraries panel. If you have Premier Pro activated for your creative cloud and Photoshop, you will have access to royalty free video stock.

To find and use Adobe Stock Video, choose Adobe Stock from the menu and enter your criteria in the search field. Click on video to narrow the results to video only, then right click the video and choose view details on the web to learn more about the details of the video you are interested in.

You will have the option to save to your library for later use, or double click the video to open it in a workspace.

Importing Your Own Digital Images

Photoshop will import your own digital images into photoshop libraries. You can import from any source; a camera, a scanner, a folder on your computer, and save to Photoshop libraries.

To import your own digital image, use the software that came with your device, then open the image with Photoshop and save to your cloud library.

You can navigate to your images once they are imported and open them in Photoshop. Once you have opened the image in Photoshop, you can save them to a library.

Open Photoshop then click windows then library, then click create new library then enter a name for the library and save. The new library is now available under libraries. You can save your images to your new library by choosing it when you click to save.

Basic Tools

Now that you know how to open an image and save an image, you can move on and familiarize yourself with the basic tools. Open an image in your work area, it can be an Adobe Stock image or an image of your own.

To learn the basics, you will use the image you have chosen.

Here is a list of the basic tools in Photoshop and their uses:

- The Rectangular Marquee Tool – the keyboard shortcut for this tool is M, or you can just click on the tool in the menu. This tool is used to select areas of your project for editing.

- The Move Tool – the keyboard shortcut is V. This tool is used to move selected layers around the work space.

- The Lasso Tool – the keyboard shortcut is L. This tool is used to create or draw a selection in any shape you want to. After you complete your selection, double click to close the selection.

- The Magic Wand Tool – the keyboard shortcut is W. This tool is used for selecting a color range. You can make your selections precise by clicking the menu for the tool. This tool selects transparency and color blocks.

- The Crop Tool – the keyboard shortcut is C. This tool will crop your image to the size you create when you hit enter/return. Anything that lies outside of the crop is now gone but you can get it back by hitting undo.

- The Healing Brush Tool – the keyboard shortcut is J.

  This tool is used to repair scratches, dust, or any other minor damage to an image. You choose a brush size then click on a part of the image undamaged and transfer the information to the damaged area and the tool blends the patch.

- The Brush Tool – the keyboard shortcut is B. This tool allows you to paint on your image using a selection of brushes, colors, and sizes.

- The Clone Stamp Tool – the keyboard shortcut is S.

  This tool clones an area of the image and allows you to move it onto another area, it works similar to the healing brush tool but it will not blend the patch.

- The Eraser Tool – the keyboard shortcut is E. This tool erases anything you drag it over on any layer that is selected.

- The Gradient Tool – the keyboard shortcut is G. This tool creates a gradient between the foreground and background colors.

- The Blur Tool – the keyboard shortcut is R. This tool blurs anything you drag it over.

- The Doge Tool – the keyboard shortcut is O. The dodge tool lightens any color you go over as long as it is not absolute black.

- The Horizontal Type Tool – the keyboard shortcut is T. This tool lets you type where you click.

- The Note Tool – the keyboard shortcut is N. This tool lets you add note boxes to your image.

- The Eyedropper Tool – the keyboard shortcut is I. This tool lets you click on a color in the image and apply it to the foreground. To change the background color click the alt key.

- The Hand Tool – the keyboard shortcut is T. This lets you grab and move your entire image around the work area.

- The Zoom Tool – the keyboard shortcut is Z. Zoom lets you zoom in to work or view.

The Crop Tool

The crop tool can crop your image permanently or you can crop then remove the crop later.

Try using the crop tool on your image; choose the crop tool from the menu and use the rectangle to choose the part of the image you want to crop to. Once you have adjusted the rectangle and are satisfied with the crop area, click crop.

The cropped image you have created can be saved to replace the original, or as a new image file.

Lighting

To adjust the lighting in your image, use the brightness/contrast tool. This tool allows you to slide the slider and adjust the brightness of your image.

This adjustment tool can lighten shadows and add contrast to washed out areas. The best way to learn how this tool affects the lighting is to work with it.

As you slide the slider, pay attention to the areas you want to lighten or darken. Moving the brightness slider to the right will lighten, dragging it to the left will darken. Once you have achieved a balance you are happy with, click on the contrast tool.

Slide the contrast slider to the right to add contrast and to the left to remove contrast. Move the slider and pay attention to your image, once you are happy with the contrast it is time to save your work.

You can save your work without changing the original by saving as a new file. Save as will allow you to save as a new image without changing the original image. The original will still be available and your new work can be saved with the changes. The save command will save your changes without saving the original image.

Removing Content

Removing content is easy once you know how it works. Open your image and click on the clone tool and choose the right sized brush for the job and set the opacity to about 95%.

Now hold down the alt button and click an area of the image that you can use to "cover" the object you want to remove.

Once you have determined the area you want to clone, release the alt button and click and drag over the object to be removed. As you drag the area you chose as a cover will follow the brush over the object. Repeat this process until the object is no longer visible.

Sharpen

Choose the image layer in the layer panel and draw around the area you want to sharpen. Once you have your area chosen, under filter, choose sharpen then unsharp mask, now you can adjust the options for your selection. When you are finished choosing options click ok and the area you selected will sharpen.

You can also use the sharpen tool on the tool panel. You can use this brush to sharpen areas that you brush. This is a tool rather than a filter, work slowly and pay attention to each result as you move the brush over your image.

 Once you are satisfied with the results you can save to save as the original or save as to save as a new image file, leaving the original untouched.

Creative Effects

Open your image and select a layer from the layer tab then double click on the layer. You will have a choice of effect options in the layer style menu. Try choosing different effect options until you find one you like.

 You can add more effects by selecting new layers and choosing different effect options in the layer style menu.

Saving Your Project

Choosing save from the save options will save the current image as it is, choosing the save as option will save your project as a separate file. You will have to name your file and choose a file format.

Choose the file format that best fits the way you use your images.

When you choose a file format, a warning will appear if your chosen format does not support all features of your project. Once you choose you file format you will have to choose a file name and a location to save.

Here is a list of options for file saving:

- Layers – this will save all the layers of your image project

- Save as a copy – this will save your work while keeping the project open for you to continue working

- Alpha Channels – this will save all of the alpha channel information along with your image

- Notes – this will save notes with the image

- Spot colors – this will save spot channel information along with the image

- Thumbnail – this will save a thumbnail of the image along with the image

Now you have enough information to use photoshop for basic digital photography tasks.

The following chapters will help you hone your skills and dig deeper into the basic tools and provide advanced information for using photoshop.

The information learned in this chapter will help you understand the advanced skills you can use while working with photoshop.

Chapter 2 – Video Editing

Photoshop provides you with the tools you need to edit video clips and create a movie, complete with audio, transitions, and titles. To begin, open your video clip in photoshop then, in the timeline window, click the + to import any remaining video you want to include.

Once you have added all of the clips you want to include in your movie, it is time to arrange them in a sequence you choose.

To arrange your clips into a sequence for your movie just click and drag them around on the timeline. Once they are in the arrangement you want you can edit the length by clipping the beginning and or ending.

You can do this by dragging the beginning or ending to the start and end points you want, or use the scissor icon to edit the length and delete any part of the clip you don't want.

To adjust the audio, click the audio icon in the upper right hand corner. From here you can mute, raise or lower the volume of individual clips or include any audio options you want.

Once you have adjusted the audio to your liking for each clip, it is time to move on to creating smart objects.

Your video has layers, click on the layers in the pallet and convert them to smart objects. Converting them to smart objects will keep them from merging. Then click on video group 1 and using the layer pallet, duplicate the video. This will add another video under the one you already have in the timeline.

Once you have duplicated the video, click on the eye to hide it from view, you don't need it just yet.

Once you have edited the clips for arrangement, size and audio, it is time to edit some details like sharpness and color grading. Click on a layer for a clip and use the tools to adjust the color gradient.

You can use the tools to adjust color gradient. The best way to do this is to make adjustments and have a look at the result.

There is no adjustment that will make your work perfect, adjustments are all about learning what you like and applying the change. Keep adjusting until you are happy with the results.

Now make that second video visible by clicking the eye icon again and apply contrast/sharpening changes to each clip on this layer. Once you have applied these changes you can merge the two videos until you are happy with the result.

You can now add new layers for text like titles and credits and adjust them the same way you adjusted the other layers. You can drag a layer to affect a small area of the video or drag it from beginning to end to affect the entire video.

Each layer is just like the layers used for digital photography. Dragging each layer allows you to decide where and how much a layer affects each clip.

Once your edits are complete, export the video by clicking file then export and render.

You can choose the rendering options for file format and photoshop will render the finished format to a folder you choose on your hard drive.

Chapter 3 – Photoshop Templates

Photoshop templates are a quick way to arrange images for web and print. You can create templates, use premade photoshop templates, or download templates.

Templates have areas for photos to be placed and they have built-in fonts and styles. Templates are available for cards, calendars, scrapbooking and more.

Find and open a template in Photoshop. Now choose the shape layer, the shape layer is the shape you want to fit your photo into, then go to file and then place, now choose the photo you want to use.

The photo will appear in the template and the photo layer will be above the shape layer.

You can resize the image you have chosen by dragging the handles. To keep image from skewing, hold down the shift key while dragging. Once you are happy with the size, go to the layer and create clipping mask, this will clip your image to the shape layer of the template.

If you need to resize after you have clipped to the shape layer, click CTRL + T for windows, or CMD + T for mac; this will make the handles visible again. Resize the image the same way you did before you created the clipping mask.

Once you are finished, go to the layer and create clipping mask again to clip the image to the shape layer.

You will follow the directions above for every picture you want to add to the template.

Click on the text layer for the template, now click on the text tool and start typing where indicated. When you are finished with your text, click the checkmark in the menu bar to save your changes.

When you are finished with your project, save it as a PSD file if you want to work with the layers in the future.

  Save in JPEG if you plan to print your project. You can work with any template you download or already have using these directions. When saving for web, choose the best format option for your web project.

Templates can help you design a magazine page, a story board, holiday cards, and many other items. Once you know how to insert images, change text, and save, you can use any template you wish, the rules are the same.

 Try working with a simple template until you get the hang of it.

Chapter 4 – Understanding Layers

Layers are simple to understand once you know what they are! A layer is used to affect changes to your original photo without changing the original. In other words, you open a photo, then add layers of changes, a layer of lighting and contrast changes, a layer of color corrections, and say, a layer of fixes.

You can then remove or continue to fine tune the layers until you have the image you want.

While working with layers you can remove one layer without affecting the others. This gives you amazing control over the edits you make.

You can add more than one change or effect to a single layer, just remember that those changes or effects will be deleted as a group if you delete the layer.

There isn't much to it, working with layers is a snap; you add layers, make changes to the layers, add to the layers, save the layers or delete the layers.

As you begin working with layers, the best way to learn is to open an image and start experimenting.

Add a layer and make some changes; remember, if you want to have the ability to delete a change without affecting the other changes, make sure you have separate layers. Spend time working with layers, making changes, adding and deleting until you get the hang of it.

You can even adjust each individual layer's effect on the image by adjusting the opacity. As you adjust the opacity you will adjust the strength of the effect on the image.

Take your time and adjust the opacity and make a mental note of the changes. Layers give you an enormous amount of control over your image without degrading the original file quality.

When you save your project, you can save it and maintain the ability to make changes to your layers, or lock them in.

If you choose a file format that will not maintain the individual layers, a warning will pop up telling you this; you can then choose to continue with the save and lose the ability to work with individual layers, or change the format and maintain the layers.

Video editing also requires layers. The same principle used for understanding layers for working with photos in Photoshop is applied to working with video in Photoshop.

Remember, nothing is final, your original images and video will remain untouched as long as you save as a new file when you save your projects.

You can apply an unlimited number of layers, you are only limited by the processing and memory of your computer. You can build up layers for effect, change the strength of an effect by changing the opacity of the layer.

Changes you make to a layer affect the image in different ways depending on the opacity, filter, and effects your choice and the arrangement of the layers.

Learning to work with Photoshop is not just about learning to use tools and techniques, it is about learning what you like and what you want to accomplish. Work with each new tool and skill set until you are proficient at achieving results you are happy with.

Learning how to apply preset changes to images and video will not give you any control over the final product; practice and patience is the only way to become awesome with photoshop!

Chapter 5 – Understanding Filters

Filters are used to create art effects, lighting effects, and retouching a photo. Filters are available from Adobe and others can be downloaded from developers un-affiliated with Adobe.

 Downloaded filters are also known as plug-ins and they will show up in the menu after they are downloaded and installed.

Filters can be applied to the entire image or to individual layers of an image project. How you apply a filter depends on the result you are looking for. All filters are useable on 8-bit images, others work for 16-bit images, and some only work on RGB images.

Some filters are for 32-bit images and others are processed using RAM. Only the filters that can be applied to the selected image will be clickable in the menu.

Smart Filters are used for Smart objects. Smart filters and smart objects allow you to apply filters without damaging the original file. Working with smart objects and filters is considered nondestructive editing.

 This is a good choice if you want to make changes and see the results without damaging or loosing information from the original file.

The following is a list of filters for 16-bit images:

- Lens Correction

- Gaussian Blur

- Liquefy

- Blur

- Blur More

- Average Blur

- Vanishing Point

- Box Blur

- Lens Blur

- Motion Blur

- Surface Blur

- Radial Blur

- Shape Blur

- Despeckle

- Add Noise

- Median

- Reduce Noise

- Dust and Scratches

- Clouds

- Fibers

- Difference Clouds

- Sharpen

- Sharpen More

- Lens Flare

- Sharpen Edges

- Smart Sharpen

- Unsharp Mask

- Solarize

- Emboss

- Find Edges

- High-Pass

This is a list of 32-bit filters:

- Gaussian Blur

- Box Blur

- Average Blur

- Motion Blur

- Radial Blur

- Shape Blur

- Surface Blur

- Add Noise

- Lens Flare

- Clouds

- Smart Sharpen

- Unsharp Mask

- Emboss

- High-Pass

The filter gallery provides a preview of filters to help you choose a filter for your project. You can use the filter gallery preview to set options, turn off, choose which filters to apply, and re-arrange the position of filters.

Once you are happy with your work in the filter gallery you can click to make the changes. The gallery helps you make changes and choose between changes by showing you how your choices affect your image.

If you want to use the gallery, click filter > filter gallery, here you will click filter category to see the available filter thumbnails. Use the hand tool to move around and drag images and use the + and − keys to zoom in or out.

You can apply a filter from the gallery preview to your image. The filters are applied to your image in the same way they were selected in the preview. Dragging the filters around in the list of used filters will change their order; this can be done after applying them.

You can hide a filter from view by clicking the eye icon and you can delete the filter from the preview by selecting and deleting a filter layer.

You can:

- Select the entire layer to use a filter on the entire image

- Select a space to use the filter in a specific space

- Use smart filters and smart objects to work non-destructively

To use a filter from the gallery on your image, click filter > filter gallery. Now click for a list of available filters then click the filter name to apply the first filter. This filter will now show up at the bottom right corner of the gallery under applied filters. Now you can choose options for your filter.

To add more filters, select the new effects icon and add another filter, repeat this to add additional filters. To change the arrangement of the position of the filters just drag them up or down in the used filters list.

Changing the position and arrangement of the filters will affect the image so look for subtle as well as obvious changes as you work with the position of the filters. Use the delete icon to remove/delete any filters you want to get rid of.

When you are happy with your choices, click ok.

You can change how long it takes to apply filters by speeding up the processing speed. Some filters use a lot of RAM to process, you can speed this up and improve the performance by previewing the filter on a small area of the entire image.

You can free up extra memory for processing filters by using the purge command. Another trick to try is to exit Photoshop and allocate more memory to the Photoshop program. Sometimes changing the settings of a filter can speed up processing.

Blend and fade effects will further change how a filter affects your image.

Fade will change the opacity and blend of a filter or painting tool; to use this option:

- Apply a filter or paint tool to the image or area

- Click edit > fade, then check the preview to see the result

- Use the slider to change the opacity anywhere from 0 – 100%

- Choose an option from the mode menu then hit ok

Another way to change the strength of a filter is to build up the effect using layers. Make sure your layer contains pixels and is visible, then apply the filter to the individual layer.

Repeat this with more layers to create a buildup of the filter effect on the image.

Try all the different filters to see how they affect your image, this is the best way to learn which filters and effects you like and why. As you work with the filters you will become accustomed to how they affect your work and you will become faster and more efficient at applying your filters.

Conclusion

Now you have the skills you need to create, edit, and produce awesome results with Photoshop. The longer you use the program, the more proficient you will become.

Remember, learning to use the tools does not make you good at editing or make you instantly creative. Your new skills will help you hone your creativity and editing skills. The more you work with Photoshop, the better you will become at using it.

Take your time and save your projects, it helps to compare your before and after images to see just how effective your changes were. You can always go back in and fine tune your projects after comparing and contrasting.

If you find you need more space for saving your work, creative cloud is a great way to add more space for saving your creations.

It takes practice but you are now on your way to mastering one of the best digital editing programs available.

www.ingramcontent.com/pod-product-compliance
Lightning Source LLC
Chambersburg PA
CBHW061233180526
45170CB00003B/1273